3 Quotes
CAN
MAKE
A
DIFFERENCE:
Plus 'Algo Mas!'

Researched and written by:
Earl O'Kuly

By The Book 4U Publishing
Brownstown, IL 62418
www.bythebook4u.com

ISBN: **978-0-9836908-4-9**

Library of Congress Headings:
Quotes
Famous people
Limits
Motivation
Beliefs
Excuses
Reasons
Results
Reframing

3 Quotes CAN Make a Difference . . .

?

Also from By the Book 4U Publishing:

"By thinking outside of the diet . . . The Melee´ Method Way to Weigh Less" by E. Nelson and Tate Tatier, show the 7 weighs to successfully losing weight, 2.5 ways to increase your metabolism and covers the top 10 reasons diets fail and ways to overcome them. It also has two bonus sections, 101 little ways to weigh less and medical reasons for weight gain. *(Available on Amazon and at your local bookstores)*

"HOH?" by Kate Carlson, a book on her experiences as a hard of hearing person, with chapters on coping skills and a final chapter on resources for the hearing impaired. *(Available on Amazon and at your local bookstores)*

"Devil at the Door" by Kate Carlson. This is the story of some of the trials and tribulations of Kate Carlson relating to what all hard of hearing people endure adjusting and adapting to this great change in their lives. Written in a light hearted and sometime humorous style it shares ways of coping with hearing impairment and it even gives the do's and don'ts for those who are 'hearing' people. This book is a must for those struggling with hearing impairment and a great book for those who interact with the hearing impaired. With a final chapter on resources this is a book to keep and use as a resource. *(Available on Amazon and at your local bookstores)*

"50 Ways to Tell a Redneck from a Hillbilly: A City Slicker's Guide to Country" by Earl O'Kuly, a book, tongue in cheek, to make you smile as he explains, from 50 down to number 1, the differences between the redneck and the hillbilly.

Based on personal experiences and anecdotes from friends and such it will take you on an interesting journey of they aren't the same, but they are kissin' cousins. *(Available on Amazon and at your local bookstores)*

3 Quotes Can Change Your Life
Set the Table of Success - Contents

Warning:

1.   Please use common sense when following the information in this book. All promises, implied or otherwise, are made on a general level and may be different for each person on an individual level.

2. Refrain from anything that you see or feel is harmful or detrimental to yourself and your life because ultimately you are the person responsible for your results.

4. Use the information in this book wisely. Your situation may not apply to everything written.

5.   No results can be guaranteed. The author nor the publisher can be held responsible for your use or results.

3 Quotes CAN Make a Difference . . .

Foreword and Forward Towards Success

Do you have a dream? A BIG DREAM? These are the dreams that tend to fall into one of two categories. The first is the DREAM that we keep hidden, deep down in the recesses of our minds, where they occasionally peek up to see if it is safe to come out. It's that crazy idea, that crazy DREAM we keep locked up in a lunatic asylum because we know crazy DREAMS should be locked up.

The second type of big DREAM is the one that comes through our mind often, and is like a wisp of a cloud, an idea, a DREAM written in smoke, reminding us often of a yearning, a hunger, sometimes an ache inside of what could be. Like a will-o-the wisp, it flits here and there through the mountains, valleys and crevices of our brain, reminding us of bigger things, better things, wonderful things. We tend to push these thoughts away, while looking the other way, with a wistful why and a wishful sigh as we slog our way through life.

It doesn't have to be because dreams can come true!

Do you know the definition of a rut? It is a grave with the ends knocked out. Although written for seniors, like me, this book is for anyone who has a DREAM and wants more out of life. It is for anyone, like you, who wants to get out of a rut.

I retired at 62, with my dream of seeing and travelling more of the world seeming farther away than ever. Yet as I sit here in Colombia, South America, having just returned from Ecuador, I am living my dream. During a week at Easter, I took a boat up the Amazon River and I trekked through the Amazon Jungle, going inland to meet with a grandfather, a shaman. It was a wonderful experience that I will treasure.

I would like to note that I came to South America with little money and almost no Spanish. I could say hi, goodbye and say 'banos por favor' to find a bathroom. That was pretty much it.

You see at one time I thought the secret was to be rich, however, when I dug down, I found what I really wanted was to travel. And that was when Henry David Thoreau's quote became more that a quote. He said, **"If one advances confidently in the direction of his dreams, and endeavors to live the life which he has imagined, he will meet with a success unexpected in common hours."**

I am finding this to be more and more true!

I wrote this book to help others, like you, go for their DREAM, to look at, to see, to feel the world in a new way. I want you to embrace life and to know, to know in your heart that this life can be better, and to know, to know you can bring your dreams to fruition!

Best wishes and may your dreams come true and success be yours, Earl O'Kuly.

PS: I saw the words, algo mas, a lot when I was in South America. It was on signs in shops and by street vendors. Loosely translated it means, 'something else'. I liken it to what we see in advertising here in the states, 'much more'. It is my hope, and my dream that you will get 'something else' from this book, that you will get 'much more' in your life by the words that I share with you. Bueno suerte! Good Luck on your journey!

'The life each of us lives is the life within the limits of our own thinking. To have life more abundant, we must think in limitless terms of abundance.' Thomas Dreier

Chapter 1

Let me start by saying the title of this book isn't true. Sometimes just one quote, one saying, can change your life, can make a difference. Want an example?

The best one I can share is this one: **'If he (or she) can do it, so can I!"** How many lives has these eight words made a difference in? I'm not sure anyone can answer that question, but it has to be a huge number.

So it doesn't matter whether you choose one, two or three, or even more quotes/sayings. It doesn't. What matters is that you decide you want more from life. You want to live your dream, have a better life's journey, then find the quote or quotes that resonate with you, within you and use them, make them a part of your life, your thinking, to follow your dreams and live the life you want.

'If he (or she) can do it, so can I!" With this, just find or read about people who have done what you want to do and emulate them.

Want to go back to school and get a high school diploma or college degree? Piece of cake because thousands and thousands of people, of all ages, have made this dream come true. Emulate them!

Want to have your own business but need your current job?   Jim Davis of Garfield fame says instead of being a moonlighter, someone who does a second business at night, become a daylighter, and work on it while at work. Crazy, right? Either way, there are thousands of people who have, either way, done it, so can you!

Find the quote or quotes that builds your fire, starts you on your journey, keeps you focused, makes you want take that first step and keep on keeping on.

It may not always be easy, but you will find it is worth it. And let us talk about what you want to accomplish. Sometimes it is just getting your car fixed and you don't have any money. As Deepak Chopra says, **"Forget about looking outside the box, get rid of the box."** I heard of a lady who needed a transmission for her car. She was a single mom with no money. She went around to transmission shops asking what they needed. All of them said they needed nothing except for one. He needed a reliable person to clean his shop each evening. They traded services and she ended up building a cleaning business and became not just self-employed, but an employer. . . and she got her transmission fixed.

So one of the secrets is to just ask. You don't ask, you never get. And this goes beyond asking others for what you want, it's about asking yourself the right questions. If you ask, 'Why does this always happen to me?' or 'Why can't I do that?' your brain will give you hundreds of answers why, all of them negative.

However, if you ask better questions, like, 'How can I do that too?' or 'What can I do right now to get started on my dream?' you will get better answers.

Think outside the box, throw out the box, and go for it!

Just yesterday my washing machine started smoking. Two weeks prior I met a lady in Missouri whose washing machine quit. She told me that when she started taking it apart her husband looked at her like she was crazy and asked her what she thought she was doing. She said she was trying to fix it, if she did, great, and if not, then it wasn't going to cost any more to have a repairman fix it. She was able to fix it.

With her story in mind, I googled my problem and found a couple of answers. An easy repair later, my washer was working again. Hmmm, my wife is saying it's her washer. Maybe I should have said 'our' washing machine.

Folks, the answers, the solutions are out there. Take losing weight. The simplest solution is to eat less, exercise more. Why, if you google dieting, you will find there are hundreds and hundreds of other ways to lose weight. All you have to do is to get into the right mindset (you might want to read the book, 'The Melee Method: The Way to Weigh Less') and find out what works for you. There is always an answer!

So what you are going to find as you continue reading is first, three quotes, dissected to help you think about what quotes can mean. Then I've included a number of more quotes with pithy comments to help you think about them. My hope is that you will find ones that get you going, going forward, not just towards your dreams, but to achieving your dreams.

Chapter 2

You miss 100% of the shots you don't take. Wayne Gretzky

This quote can reach out and touch us on many levels. The first level, no matter what you think of Nike©, is the 'Just Do It!' level. When we truly want something, really want something, we move heaven and earth, going over, under, around or through any problems, any obstacles to achieve our desire.

Alas, this doesn't happen nearly often enough. What happens way too often is we find a reason or reasons why not to do something . . . however what we often find if we unwrap reasons is that they are just excuses wrapped up in a pretty package. It behooves us to do something called looking outside the box, to unwrap excuses, I mean reasons, to not see if they are true, but to see if they can be overcome some way, somehow.

Then there is the 'other' level, the belief level. This somewhat tied to the prior level, the reason or excuse level, however the belief level is at a much deeper, and much stronger level inside of us.

Excerpt from the book, 'The Melee Method Way to Weigh Less':

*'You may or may not have heard of Roger Bannister and his story. Briefly it goes like this: going back in time, the early '50s, there was a belief the mile could not be ran in less than 4 minutes. That belief was supported by doctors and other experts who purported, beyond a shadow of a doubt that it was physically impossible to run the mile in under 4 minutes. However, with less training and pre-work than we see today, on May 6th, 1954, Roger Bannister proved that belief wrong when he broke the 4 minute record, running the mile in 3 minutes 59.4 seconds. Amazing, wasn't it? However, **that is not the most amazing part of the story.** Once he proved it could be done, within 3 years 16 others went on to run the mile in under 4 minutes! Hmmm, after years of trying did all of these people's bodies change? NO! What happened is their belief systems changed. Note: Many doctors and researchers of their day irrefutably documented that it was impossible to run*

a 4 minute mile. Hah! Do not believe the 'experts'.

Over and over there are stories like this, that once the mental obstacle, the obstacle of belief has been overcome, people can then overcome all of the 'other' obstacles when committed to achieving a dream, a goal, a desire. Belief! Don't start your dream without it!!!!'

Believe in yourself and believe in your dreams!

How about the comfort zone level?   We become ensconced in our habits and this is just the way it is'. This one has an easy fix, just get off of your buts! But I'm too old, but I'm too young, but don't have the money, but I don't have the time, but I've never done it before, but what will people say/think . . . get off of those 'buts' and make your dreams happen!

The last level to think about is the fear level. There's the fear of failure, the fear of success, the fear of looking foolish and on and on and on.   Unwrap these, dig deep, because the odds are in your favor they are more like excuses.   There is a book by

Susan Jeffers, 'Feel the Fear And Do It Anyway'. Read the book, or not, just get up and make positive things happen in your life.

If you think you can, or if you think you can't, you're probably right. Henry Ford

Close your left eye, notice that you now see your nose.

Close your right eye, hmmm, again you see your nose.

So why don't you see your nose when both eyes are open? Our brain plays tricks on us. We do it to ourselves. We see what we want to see, and conversely, don't see what we don't want to see. The same with hearing, and the same with believing, hence the word dogmatism.

Have you ever said, "I could never do that." Why? What's stopping you? I chose to reframe 'looking foolish' to 'having fun' and it has changed my life. I've learned to laugh at myself. Guess what? You can do this and more when you decide you want to live an 'I can life' rather than an 'I can't life.' Your choice.

3 Quotes CAN Make a Difference . . .

Great minds discuss ideas; average minds discuss events; small minds discuss people. Eleanor Roosevelt

Quit gossiping and worrying about what others say about you . . . it doesn't matter. She also said, **"No one can make you feel inferior without your consent."**

Another of her quotes, **"The future belongs to those who believe in the beauty of their dreams."**

It's said you are most like the five people you spend the most time with. Are you hanging with winners or losers?

When I was in South America most of the volunteers were young people, many fresh from college. They let me hang with them and it was a life changing experience. They stretched my boundaries and made me think in different ways. They had me going to new places and trying new things. When I returned I found most folk my age were set in their ways, from the food they ate to the way they lived their lives.

I once called a lady to tell her I had setup a job interview for her. Her daughter answered the phone and I asked her to get her mom so I could arrange a job interview for her. The young girl came back to the phone and told me her mom couldn't come to the phone because Oprah was on. How sad that someone could let TV become more important than a life changing experience. TV is but bubblegum for the brain, don't do it. By the way, do you think Oprah would have let watching a TV show stop her from a life changing experience? Her life proves otherwise, doesn't it?

When you open your mind to new ideas you open your life to new options, to the possibility of dreams coming true.

What does this mean for you?

We've dissected 3 quotes, but these might not be the right quotes for you. The point of doing this was to get you thinking, to get you off of your 'buts' and to look at and unwrap those things that are stopping you, that are holding you back.

The idea is for you to find 3 quotes that help you on YOUR journey to making your dreams come true. One quote, if it truly motivates you, keeps you on track and helps you open your mind and open doors will do the job.

With that in mind, I will touch on some more quotes to help you on your journey.

Chapter 3

It is never too late to be what you might have been. –George Eliot

To say it's too late is an excuse. Every day you wake up is a new day. A new day for you to start over, to start towards who you want to be.

I've started over many times in my life. Sometimes it is just new clothes, a different look. Many times it has been a new job, new people, new experiences. And yes, it has been moving to another country.

Mostly though, regardless of the circumstances, it has been an attitude adjustment. Thinking differently can make all the difference in the world!

The happiest people I know are always evaluating and improving themselves. Unhappy people are usually evaluating and judging others. Lisa V. Prosen

Note that this says evaluating, not criticizing yourself. Big difference!

Have you ever heard of the Pareto Principle, sometimes called the 80/20 Rule? It is a rule of thumb that states that 80% of outcomes can be attributed to 20% of all causes for a given event.

For this the best example is your closet. More likely than not you wear 20% of your clothes 80% of the time and 80% of your clothes 20% of the time.

This means a number of things. One, you probably don't need all of the clothes in your closet. Oh yes, and it also means you don't need all of the excess baggage you are carrying around in your brain.

Did you know it means that you don't need to make a complete makeover to improve your life. Just find the 20% changes that will give you 80% of the results that you want to achieve.

Some examples of things you can do that will give you big benefits:

- Research has shown repeatedly that meditation can bring about many benefits
- Exercise, not only to lose weight and look better, gives you more energy and makes you feel better about yourself.
- Reframing, changing how you look or feel about something or someone can help you build a better life by leaps and bounds.

Let me share two reframes, in one day, that happened to me.   When I was working in Chicago, I received an unsolicited sales call and of course I didn't buy, but at the end of it the young lady told me to have a nice day. I unloaded on her. I vented my day: On the way to work I was run off the road and spilled coffee all over my shirt. When I got to work I had to go down the street and buy a new one for a meeting that ended up being cancelled. When I went to get my lunch from the fridge it was missing. I went to my car to go out, but found out my keys were locked in the car. I walked down the street for lunch. I told her it was too late for a good day. She said, "Wow, you had a great day!" Incredulously I had to ask her how she figured that. She proceeded to tell me that I didn't get into an accident and I got a new shirt didn't I? I got a hot lunch. And I'm in Chicago, the keys are in my car and it didn't get stolen. It was a great day! I laughed and agreed with her. Major reframe!

However, I decided rather than pay a locksmith, I would take the train home, get my motorcycle and return to move my car to a safer parking place, then return to work tomorrow by train. I get home. Before I can take off though I get a phone call from a friend who tells me the bridge out of town is closed. So now I'm going to have to take the long way. No biggie. However on my way out of town a kid on a bicycle turns in front of me and I have to lay my bike down. I barely get missed from being run over by a minivan. My windshield is broken. I ride back home and remove it, get glasses to be legal and take off again. By the time I finally get back home it's almost ten o'clock at night and I am grumpy again and past ready for bed. But my son meets at the door and says, "Dad, don't be mad." You know that means bad news. It seems he hasn't been placing the trash in the trash cans, but has been setting the bags outside the back porch and now something is living in there. So I stand guard with a shovel over my shoulder while he slowly moves trash bags of garbage. I'm expecting a possum, maybe a rat. My son keeps moving garbage. We hear scuffling, but haven't seen anything. Now we're down to the last bag. He quickly moves it. Something moves, I start to swing, stop and jump back, <u>way back</u> as a baby skunk waddles away alongside the house. A bad day just became a great day, an awesome day, because any day you don't get sprayed by a skunk is a wonderful day! All of the bad things became meaningless and the day ended up very positive.

Another example was when I was pickpocketed in Bogotá, Colombia. My money, my credit cards, my ID . . . gone. I had to walk 77 long blocks to get to where I could find help. I could have moaned, complained and cried over spilt milk. However, none of that would have brought my billfold and my belongings back. So I decided to see how many people I could make laugh with me about it. I could have looked at it as a horrible experience or I could call it part of the adventure.

Adventure? Oh yeah! It was worth it just to be able to be in South America. Reframe how you look at things and you change your life!

I would like to note the volunteers who looked for the positives and made lemonade from the negatives had far more fun than the whiners and complainers.

At any moment you have the power to say this is not how the story is going to end, don't you?

Some people look at life as a painter's canvas with each new day being painted in with the pictures and colors they choose. Of course there are many people who let others paint their canvas, then complain when it doesn't turn out the way they desire.

There are others who see life as a garden. Some folks let their garden go and it becomes weed infested. They tend to whine and complain about life. Then there are the folk who till and plant and tend to their garden with positives and enjoy the fruits of their labors and truly enjoy life.

Who is writing your story? Make it YOU!

If it is important to you, you will find a way, If not you will find an excuse. unknown

We've covered this. Check your reasons, because more often than not they are just excuses wrapped up pretty. However, no matter how pretty they are wrapped, they should be unwrapped and overcome. If you're breathing, it means you are an overcomer. Think of all the things you have overcome to still be alive today.

If plan A doesn't work, remember, there are 25 more letters in the alphabet – 204 if you're in Japan.
Claire Cook

Can you say, where there's a will, there's a way?

To quote Winston Churchill, **"Never, never, never give up!"**

Can you say, go over, under, around, or through to reach your goal, your dream?

When you give up, it's over. And remember, it's often the journey, rather than the destination that makes the experience.

It's all about getting up, over and over and over, never giving up, and moving forward until you reach your destination, achieve your dream.

Life is like a camera, focus on what's important and capture the good times, develop from the negatives, and if things don't work out, just take another shot. unknown

This one is pretty explanatory. It's all about reframing, about how you think, how you look at things, choosing how you feel.

You can't live a positive life with a negative mind. Excerpt from a larger quote by Miley Cyrus. *(I would have never guessed when I was looking up where some of my quotes came from that I would have one by Miley Cyrus. I guess I need to open my mind up even more, eh?)*

Okay, so maybe I'm harping a bit too much on this positive attitude thing. Then again, maybe not. Reframing and staying positive, though not Polianna, truly changes things. Think about it, optimists and pessimists experience the same things. However the optimists enjoy life more.

Forget all the reasons why it won't work . . , and believe the one reason it will. Jelly Wong, from his list of wisest sayings

Ahhh, look closely, this is just another way of saying what has already been said.

Think about it, you have a hundred reasons why you shouldn't go for it, but when you have one powerful reason to go for it, one strong desire to make your dream come true, that's all you need.

Desire, a strong desire, brings about wonderful, fantastic things. A strong desire brings you opportunities. A strong desire can bring about miracles . . . if you let it.

Here's another quote saying the same thing:
It takes but one positive thought when given a chance to survive and thrive to overpower an entire army of negative thoughts. Robert H. Schuller

Keep thinking, build desire, and take that first step and go for it!

Life is like a roller coaster. It has its ups and downs. But it is your choice to scream OR enjoy the ride. unknown

It's all about the choices you make and the way you look at things.

Does life has its ups and downs? Mine does. Back when my house flooded I didn't have flood insurance. Tens of thousands of dollars in damages, so I went out and got three part-time jobs besides my fulltime job.

One of the jobs was as a security guard. Most of the other people doing this job whined and complained. Some people looked down on me for doing it. But you know what? I used that time to write and market my first book. I didn't get rich, but I made $800 and I had the satisfaction of having written and published a book. Lots of people talk about writing a book . . . I did it.

The thing of it is, so can you. Take those lemons and make lemonade my friend.

Instead of thinking outside the box, get rid of the box. Deepak Chopra

Is this a reframe OR a paradigm shift?

This quote, all by itself, opens the door to options, to possibilities.

Want an example? I was always looking for ways to make money so I could travel. But even when I did, something would always come up that required me to use the money for something else.

This became the dream that was the wisp of a cloud, the idea, the DREAM written in smoke, the yearning, the hunger, sometimes an ache inside of me for what could be.

Then came an opportunity to help setup and run a vocational school in Ghana if the contract came through. But it didn't.

However, from my research into that I found out about TEFL, Teaching English as a Foreign Language. I found a school online and got my certificate.   I then researched openings and came across the one in Colombia where they walked you through the whole visa, banking and finding a place to live process. The rest is history, is memories and friends I will cherish forever.

Very seldom will your path be straight from point A to point B. It will meander here and there, have its ups and downs, and I promise there will be challenges. I will also promise the journey is worth it when you do reach your goal, your dream and you have your memories of an awesome achievement.

Thinking outside of the box is a good start, but when you throw the box away and look at life from a different perspective, from a different reframe, you truly start living, start living your dream, living the life you thought wasn't possible. Go for it!!!

It takes as much energy to wish as it does to plan. Eleanor Roosevelt

It is good to dream, but dreams without a plan, without action is nothing more than wishing. You have to, you must, you 'gotta' have a plan and take that first step.   Remember, if someone else has done it, you can too!

Have I said how much I love this lady and would have loved to have met her. I could write a book just using her quotes.

Chapter 4

Attitude is the difference between an ordeal and an adventure. Unknown, but came, again, from Jelly Wong's list

I can guarantee you that a positive attitude is the key that opens the doors of opportunity.

Maybe this is a way of saying reframing is an attitude adjustment. Hmm, just thinking.

It is not your aptitude, but your attitude, that determines your altitude. Zig Ziglar

I thought I would throw another quote in with the first one to strengthen the power of attitude.

Now if you are going to win the any battle, you are going to have to do one thing. You are going to have to get the mind to run the body. Never let the body tell the mind what to do. The body will always give up. It is always tired in the morning, noon, and night. But the body is never tired if the mind is not tired. George S. Patton

Rather long, but definitely makes you think, now doesn't it?

Have you ever come home from work, just sat down and not wanted to get up? We all have. However, have you been home, tired and maybe even a bit cranky, when a friend calls you? Your friend says there's a sale going on and something you wanted, a sweater, a coat, a pair of boots, something you really, really wanted, just came on sale, 50% off and now you can afford it.

You jump up, excited, and away you go, on your way to making a dream come true.

What happened? You were tired, you didn't want to get up, you didn't want to move, but then you became excited, energized, motivated and moving. What changed? What changed? Just your thoughts. Now go back reread the quote above, and look at it and feel the difference, grasp the meaning. Take control my friend, take control.

Life is simple, if are you happy then keep going; if you are unhappy, then change something. unknown

My quote when I have a problem in my life is this: **Fix it, change it, or live with it.**

The classic example is a marriage. Can it be fixed? If not, is divorce (change it) the right answer? Or, is it really not so bad when you really think about it, and you can live with it?

I heard a saying, 'Women get married thinking he will change, and men get married thinking things won't change and they're both wrong!'

From the counseling I've done and the people I've met, what I have found is that, when you get back to the reason(s) you became married, you find the marriage can either be fixed, or things really aren't that bad and you can live with him or her. When marriages fail and divorce is the answer, usually but not always, it involves infidelity. Sad but true.

Whatever the mind of man can conceive and believe, it can achieve. –Napoleon Hill

This goes back to the second quote, at the beginning of the book, by Henry Ford. Think about it.

Two roads diverged in a wood, and I took the one less traveled by, and that has made all the difference. – Robert Frost

It's great to learn from other people's experiences, both good and bad. However, on the flip side, never let the naysayers keep you from your journey, from your dreams.

When I told folks I was going to Colombia South America, they told me I was crazy. However, when I started posting pictures and talking about my experiences on Facebook, they changed their tune, many of them saying they now wished they were down there with me.

Once someone else has done something, it becomes easier for others to follow. If I can do it, you can too. Not just travelling, but writing a book. Follow your dreams!

Remember, even on roads less travelled there has been someone who has gone down that path, that road. Find them, emulate them, make your dreams come true.

I attribute my success to this: I never gave or took any excuse. – Florence Nightingale

Don't go through life giving or taking excuses or living with reasons that are nothing more than excuses wrapped up in a pretty package. Tear the wrapping off, see it for what it really is, and get out there and have fun, make positive things happen. Go for it!!!

I've missed more than 9000 shots in my career. I've lost almost 300 games. 26 times I've been trusted to take the game winning shot and missed. I've failed over and over and over again in my life. And that is why I succeed. –Michael Jordan

I like to remind myself of this quote by Michael Jordan when I can't seem to get things to go right. It helps.

If you didn't know who Michael Jordan is and you saw these stats, you would think LOSER! However, we both know, Michael Jordan was and is a WINNER, and yes, WINNER spelled with capital letters.

Like riding a bicycle, you don't just get on and go. It's a learning experience. Well most things in life are the same. You fall down, you get up and you keep doing it until you get it right.

Remember that feeling of your legs pumping, the wind in your face, and of going fast on your bicycle? Oh yeah! It's worth it my friend, it's worth it!

The most difficult thing is the decision to act, the rest is merely tenacity. –Emelia Earhart

Confucius said that a journey of a thousand miles begins with a single step. Until you take action, that first step, nothing happens . . . ever.

Begin!

Definiteness of purpose is the starting point of all achievement. – W. Clement Stone

I was fortunate enough to have met this man. I'm short, he was shorter, but he was dynamic. He would be walking along and jump up and say, "I feel healthy, I feel happy, I feel TERRIFIC!"

He not only stayed focused, he was an exceptional problem solver. He was always looking for solutions, never dwelling on problems or why they happened.

Think about where you want to go, decide, then get out there and find ways, make ways, to get there.

We become what we think about. –
Earl Nightingale

This goes back to the first Eleanor
Roosevelt quote at the beginning of the
book. Choose your thoughts and in so
doing get rid of the negative thoughts.

Grandma Moses put it this way: **Life is what we make it, always has been, always will be.**

Twenty years from now you will be more disappointed by the things that you didn't do than by the ones you did do, so throw off the bowlines, sail away from safe harbor, catch the trade winds in your sails. Explore, Dream, Discover. –Mark Twain

Life is what we make it. Do I regret some of the things I did? You bet. However, I have many more regrets of things I didn't do. I'm trying to make up for that and I'm writing this book to help you too. Explore, dream, discover!!!

Life is 10% what happens to me and 90% of how I react to it. – Charles Swindoll

Reframing and attitude . . . again!

Chapter 5

The most common way people give up their power is by thinking they don't have any. –Alice Walker

You always have power. More than you know. We all have untapped potential.

One of my favorite stories is about an author who was writing a book on peak performance, he even titled the book by that. One day he read about an elderly lady in Florida who was babysitting her grandchildren. She was standing at the kitchen sink when she looked out the window and saw one the children had taken the car out of gear and she watched as it rolled onto her favorite grandchild. She ran out the door. She ran to the back of the car. She not only stopped it, she picked it up so the child could be pulled out. That evening five big construction workers, who had heard the story, came by and tried to pick up the back of that car. It was one of those old, boat of a cars, and they couldn't get the tires even close to leaving the ground.

The author called the lady to talk to her about the incident, but she refused to talk about it. However, sometime later he was in Florida in a rental car with unlimited mileage so he decided to drive to her home to see if he could convince her to talk with him. He knocked on the door. The elderly lady answered, but then told him she didn't want to talk about 'the incident'. However, she said since he had driven so far he could come in for some fresh lemonade. They sat in the kitchen and talked, but she adamantly refused to talk about what happened. He finally asked her why she wouldn't talk about 'the incident'. She looked up at him with sad eyes and her voice quivered as she replied, "Because how much more could I have accomplished in my life if I had known I could pick up the back of a car?"

He asked her if she could do or be anything what would it be and she replied she had a love of rocks and would love to teach it to others. He said why don't you and she said because she was too old. He looked at her and told her in four years she would be four years older, with, or without, a degree to teach her love of rocks. She went back to school and now teaches her love of rocks to others.

I may have some of the details wrong, but the gist of it is correct. And you, you become another year older each and every year, living or not living your dreams. Get up, right now, and take that first step . . . and keep on going my friend, keep on going.

The mind is everything. What you think you become. —Buddha

We've covered this, probably more than once. However, it is worth seeing again in a different quote.

Here is another excerpt from the book, 'The Melee Method Way to Weigh Less': *The best way to describe the thought process . . . to think about a yard you've seen that was well maintained with flowers and shrubs, landscaped to make the yard a beautiful sight/site. Do you have it pictured?*

Now look around until you feel you have found just the opposite, a yard or maybe a vacant lot that is filled with weeds, that hasn't been mowed and just looks and feels...feels scrubby, dirty, that is an eyesore. Did you find one?

Think about the two. One is tended and cared for, but the other, well, weeds grow without any help and they can overcome a yard rather quickly if left alone.

Two ends of the spectrum, right? Now compare these, this concept, and think about your brain. Think about how you care for it, how you tend to it. What nutrients (positives) are you feeding it? What weeds (negatives) are you pulling out? What flowers (positive, achieving stories) are you planting? What toxins (negative books, negative TV, negative people) are you removing to ensure the growth of the positives? Are you letting light in? If a flower (positive) dies for any reason, are you immediately removing it and planting a new flower (positive story, uplifting thought, etc.)? If yes, GREAT! If not, why not?

Whatever you can do, or dream you can, begin it. Boldness has genius, power and magic in it. – Johann Wolfgang von Goethe

When I decided to be a volunteer and teach English in a foreign country I thought it would be Mexico. I searched the internet, for hours, looking for opportunities. It wasn't until I saw an opportunity in Colombia for the third time that I made contact with the group in Colombia. But once I did, everything came together like it was meant to be. Even when I got there, things just came together. It was unbelievable.

A simpler example was when I wanted a laptop for my part-time marketing-consulting business. The problem was I didn't have the money at the time to buy one. However I put it out to the universe. I did my daily affirmations. I put a timeline of 30 days on it. At the end of 30 days, no laptop. I gave it 30 more days. I put more feelings into my desire. Sometime during the third week a friend brought me a catalog, and in it were laptops for sale. However she reminded me I didn't have the money for a laptop. I took the catalog. As I was reading it I saw where they would let me buy one by making 3 payments. Hey, I could do that. Before the end of the second 30 days I had my laptop.

If you want something, really want it, you can and you will find a way to make it happen. The answers are out there, and my friend, the answers are often within you. Be bold, be magical, be a dreamer who is a doer!

Taking action, with a strong desire and a never give up attitude can, and will, make positive things happen. unknown

Here it is again: strong desire – taking action. I've heard so many people who failed saying, "Yeah, I didn't think I would make it."

How can you make it, how can you win with an attitude of defeat? Here in America we love the underdog, the person who overcomes massive obstacles to win. Almost all of them had a strong desire and they took action, sometimes massive action to succeed.

When Mother Theresa wanted to start an orphanage in India, people laughed at her. Those who knew her told her she only had something like $2, so there was no way she could make it happen.

She replied, "You're right. With just $2 I can't do it, but with God and $2 I can do anything!"

I'm not pushing God. What I am pushing is that with a strong desire, take action and make your dreams come true!!!

People often say that motivation doesn't last. Well, neither does bathing. That's why we recommend it daily. –Zig Ziglar

I met Zig briefly where I met W. Clement Stone the first time. I wish I had heard him say this sooner in my life. The negatives come at you with no assistance, but positives need to be planted like annuals, again and again and again. And they need to be taken care of, often, so they blossom and bloom.

Research has shown that we are bombarded by negatives, over and over and over. We need, we must, we have to work, every day on staying positive, finding the good, smelling the flowers.

I don't know what will work for you. You need to do that. So just do it, make it happen!

Life shrinks or expands in proportion to one's courage. –Anais Nin

What is courage? The dictionary defines it as: the quality of mind or spirit that enables a person to face difficulty, danger, pain, etc., without fear; bravery.

I disagree with the part about without fear. For many of us it means going for our dreams in spite of the fear. Do you think I wasn't scared of going to a foreign country where I didn't know the language? Was it a struggle when I got there? Oh yeah! Was it worth it? A thousand times yes!

They say 80% of what we fear never happens. And the 20% that does, well, we make it through it, don't we?

Do bad things happen? Yes, but we work through them and get on with our lives.

Ask and it will be given to you; search, and you will find; knock and the door will be opened for you. –Jesus

Not quite the King James version, but still, this verse resonates with Christians and even non-Christians.

Do you know how many people don't get what they want because they didn't ask? If you don't ask you never get. It's that simple.

Then there are the people who are offered what they want, but turn it down. I've been guilty of both.. I'm getting better at this though.

Did you know Shakespeare helped write the King James Version? I've often wondered, because he liked to play on words, if he didn't have a hand in this verse because of Ask, Seek and Knock, the first letters make ASK.

The only person you are destined to become is the person you decide to be. –Ralph Waldo Emerson

It is said our lives are made up of the choices we make. To change our lives it behooves us, no requires us, to make better choices.

When I first moved to Chicago I remember hearing people there constantly saying 'what goes around, comes around.' The Good Book says to treat others the way you want to be treated. There are so many sayings that allude to this, which can be summed up in one word: Karma.

I have found as I grow older, that the more I walk in love, look for the good things, stop to smell the flowers, appreciate the blessings I have, the more wonderful my life is. It's amazing how that works.

I have found that overlooking things, especially those that don't really matter, biting my tongue, have helped me have more friends and a much happier life. Note: I do stand up to those things, and for those things, that matter.

Folks, I can't emphasize enough the power of this. I once managed a group of people in a call center. I had one young lady who I had to constantly talk to about being nicer to our customers. Then one day I overheard her talking right after she had made a personal phone call. She was complaining about how rude the person she was talking to was to her. I saw an opportunity. I sat her down and explained to her that she was doing the same things as the person she was complaining about. It was an eye opening experience for her. She went on to become a mentor to others.

You need to look at who you are, your thoughts, your actions and how you look at and treat others. Then decide if this is who you really want to be.

Let me share another example. My wife is always late to the point she will probably be late for her own funeral. I've even seen her get up early so she would be on time, and then be late. This bothered me when we first married, bothered me a lot. However, when I thought about it, it hit me that if I loved her, truly loved her, then I should love every aspect of her, even this. It no longer bothers me because I changed how I look at it, how I look at her and how I feel and it has made all the difference in the world, in our marriage.

Decide, try these ideas and find the difference it can make in your life.

Keep your face to the sunshine and you cannot see the shadow. It's what sunflowers do. Helen Keller

Near where I lived, one summer, a farmer planted acres and acres and acres of sunflowers, and in the mornings they were all facing east, watching the sunrise. In the afternoons and evenings they were facing west, taking in the last rays of the sunset. This was one of my most beautiful and treasured memories. Life is about following the sunshine, seeing and feeling the beauty of life.

Life takes on meaning when you become motivated, set goals and charge after them in an unstoppable manner. Les Brown

Les Brown is another person I was fortunate enough to meet. Talk about an awesome, dynamic person, he's amazing.

I first heard about and met Les through a VHS tape I was given. It sat around my house for three or four months, then one day I was stuffing envelopes and put it on to watch while did this very boring, repetitious job. The title was, 'You've Got To Be Hungry.' I was hooked and made a goal to meet this man.

They say we are but six degrees of separation from anyone. This means if you put your request to meet someone to EVERYONE you know and ask them to ask everyone they know, six people down the chain, one of them knows the person you want to meet.

So I put this out there. I found one person who had a family member who worked for Oprah and Les Brown was on the show sometimes. Good lead for me. One of my students went to a church in Chicago that

Les Brown talked at sometimes. Good lead for me. I kept asking people, telling everyone I wanted to meet Les Brown.

Did any of these bear fruition? Nope. However, a friend saw where Les was doing a book signing. I gave up a superbowl party, at my house no less, to meet Les Brown. I stayed at the end of the line, always letting others go ahead of me. At the end, I was the last person and was able to spend some quality time getting to meet and know the man.

I share this to show that when you set a goal and go for it, with a strong desire, you can make things happen. Just don't be surprised when they come about in ways you didn't imagine.

PS: If you ever have a chance to meet Les Brown, do it. The man is down to earth and yet is amazing.

Chapter 6

"Life is either a daring adventure or nothing" – Helen Keller

The flip side quote: **The mass of men lead lives of quiet desperation.** Henry David Thoreau

I've been there. Quivering, shaking inside of my comfort zone, looking out at possibilities, at opportunities, at adventures and I turned around and hid behind my fears.

Yeah, I've been there, but I decided that a comfort zone is a cage and I have refused to be caged. Life is for living, not just surviving.

There <u>are</u> answers, there <u>are</u> ways to go over, under, around and/or through obstacles, impossibilities to live, really live!

Have you heard the story of the couple, I believe from Chicago, who had a friend coming in from Kansas City to visit. When he arrived they took him to their favorite restaurant for dinner. They told him the food there was great. He asked if the fried chicken was good. They said they didn't know because they hadn't tried it. He asked if the lasagna was good. They said they didn't know because they hadn't tried it. He asked about a couple of other menu items with the same answer. The wife said she always had the ribeye steak and the husband said he always had the meatloaf. Their friend said to them that they didn't know if the food was really good there except for what they always had. So they decided to each order something different and share to check out other foods.

After their friend left, they looked at each other and came to the conclusion they were living in a rut. They decided to expand their horizons. They started trying new restaurants. One of the restaurants had ballroom dancing. It looked like fun so they took lessons and found out they were very good at it. They entered dance contests and started winning. They were so good they were invited to dance in France, all expenses paid.

Open your mind, open your heart and open new doors!

"I have not failed. I've just found 10,000 ways that won't work." – Thomas Edison

An awesome reframe. Reframing is a tool, a skill, that can and will change your life and allow you to see things in a more positive way.

In talking about not failing, never giving up, remember Colonel Sanders. At 65, receiving his first social security check, he said he couldn't live like this. He figured out his one major asset, a family chicken recipe, and decided to sell it. Here was a senior citizen who lived in his car, primarily living on fried chicken, going from restaurant to restaurant. Some say he went to over 1,000 restaurants before he made his first sale. Yet his name has become world famous.

Can you, will you, keep on keeping on? Because most people quit at the first no. A number of people quit at the second no. Most of the rest quit at the third no. BUT that small percent that keeps on keeping on are the ones who move on to change their lives!

"A man can fail many times, but he isn't a failure until he begins to blame somebody else" – John Burroughs

Sometimes things happen beyond our control. How we choose to live with it makes all the difference. We choose to be either victims, survivors or we can choose to be winners. It's a choice, choose wisely!

Chapter 7

When you take charge of your life, there is no longer a need to ask permission of other people or society at large. When you ask permission, you give someone veto power over your life. Geoffrey F. Abert

Until we move out of our parent's house, we must live by their rules. However, it is my belief that we make choices even at an early age that impacts our future life. We are constantly making choices.

So as we get older and older, we have to live with prior choices, but we can make new choices to change, to enhance our life's experiences.

Don't want to exercise? Take up dancing and have fun staying fit.

No money for what you want? Learn to barter, to trade what you do have for what you want.

One of my mantras is that it is it is easier to ask forgiveness than to ask permission.

(Be careful how you use this one, it has backfired on me a couple of times.)

Bottom line, when you take control of your life, when you take responsibility for your choices and your actions, you start living.

Go confidently in the direction of your dreams. Live the life you have imagined. –Henry David Thoreau

Believe you can and you're halfway there. –Theodore Roosevelt

Limitations live only in our minds. But if we use our imaginations, our possibilities become limitless. –Jamie Paolinetti

Lets do a threefer because all three of these are saying the same thing.

Belief will make or break you. Our brains have limits, but our minds have no limits. The only limitations are those we impose.

Our brains have a limited IQ. And within this, IQ means very little on whether a person is or isn't successful. What counts is our desire, how strong this emotion is and whether we are willing to overcome our fear(s) to take action, to move forward.

Believe, be an overcomer, and go for it!

When I was 5 years old, my mother always told me that happiness was the key to life. When I went to school, they asked me what I wanted to be when I grew up. I wrote down 'happy'. They told me I didn't understand the assignment, and I told them they didn't understand life. –John Lennon

Along with this, I love this quote by Abraham Lincoln: **Most people are about as happy as they make up their mind to be.**

There are some people who are happy being martyrs. Let's not you and me be martyrs. I'm like, "why cry over spilt milk." Doesn't bring the milk back, now does it?

I've a lot of aches and pains. Some due to age, many due to accidents, mostly motorcycle. I could use these to not enjoy life, to sit around and moan and complain. It's a choice. I could choose to use this as an excuse, as a reason, but I didn't. I walked kilometers around a scenic volcano outside of Otavalo, Ecuador, while on a cane. Did it hurt.

Yes it did! Was it worth it? A thousand times yes. It was a beautiful, fantastic journey.

Regardless of the fears, of the pain, of the obstacles, I choose to live. Choose to live my friend, choose to live.

Everything you've ever wanted is on the other side of fear. –George Addair

I mentioned this book before, 'Feel the Fear and Do It Anyway.' I'm not going to say fears aren't real. I'm not going to say they are groundless. What I am going to say to you is to not let them hold you back.

Let's take fear of flying. There was a time when my fingerprints were embedded on the seat handles of a number of commercial airplanes. There was no way I was getting on a non-commercial plane, right? I would drive thousands of miles a month to avoid flying.

The VP of the company I worked for came to me and told me I would not be promoted above my current level unless I could overcome this problem.

First, you have to understand I wanted that promotion. I wanted it bad! I looked at ways to overcome my fear: drugs, hypnosis, willpower. However, a person close to me suggested I take flying lessons. I decided to give it a try. Not only did I find I enjoyed flying, I found out I wasn't afraid of flying, I was afraid of not being in control. Learning to take control of a plane, learning aerodynamics, helped me overcome my fear.

Desire, strong desire for the promotion and the willingness to take action, even an action that scared the heck out of me, changed my life. I now fly every chance I get. Why, since that time I once even owned a gyrocopter and was working towards my sports pilot license for it. Amazing how life works when you open your mind, isn't it?

You may be disappointed if you fail, but you are doomed if you don't try. –Beverly Sills

Folks, this goes back to the very first quote in the book by Wayne Gretzky, **You miss 100% of the shots you don't make.**

I like to look at worst case scenarios and best case scenarios when trying to decide whether to go for my goal.

My best example would be when deciding to go to Colombia as a volunteer. Worst case to me was that would either become so ill I would have to come home or just not like it and have to come home. (Note: I did my research and found the odds of dying or getting killed were so minimal as to not be counted.) I then looked at the best case scenario, which was to enjoy volunteering and see new sights.

Most of the time you end up coming up somewhere in the middle. However, in this instance I ended up surpassing my best case scenario. I fell in love with my students, many of whom I still remain in contact with. I went to places and saw sights most people in the world will never see.

Kick Mr. Doom and Gloom out of your life, out of your brain, out of your mind, out of your thoughts, and know, even if you fail, you will have memories, you will have adventures in your life.

Don't be a spectator to life, live it my friend, live it!

You can't use up creativity. The more you use, the more you have. – Maya Angelou

This is one smart lady! Don't think you're creative? How about a problem solver? We are all creative problem solvers, have been from the day we were born. Learned to walk didn't you?

However, instead of living from paycheck to paycheck, become creative, become a problem solver to be more, do more, live more!

Ask the right question: How can I make this happen?

OR

Look at the end result, then work backwards to where you are at now to build a plan to make your dream come true.

OR

Find someone or someones who have done what you want to do and emulate them.

Yeah, I know 'someones' is not a real word, but I like it for this message.

The way I see it, if you want the rainbow, you gotta put up with the rain. - Dolly Parton

I love rainbows. I have seen a lot of them. I've seen doubles and even a few triple rainbows. They are beautiful scenes of nature.

So am I willing to put up with some rain? You bet!

Nowhere have I said it will be easy. I have said it is worth it to go for your dreams. I have said when you have a strong desire, and you take action, things will come together. I believe that.

I can guarantee you won't get it by whining and complaining. Even other whiners and complainers don't like whiners and complainers.

I can also tell you procrastinators don't get it. Along with that, I did not say to not have patience nor that it would not take time.

I put out to the universe I needed a car. I was driving a '98 pickup with over

240,000 miles on it. I was often doing over 200 miles a day. It took me <u>six months</u> to find my car. Was it worth it. Oh yeah! I found a one owner, with only 88,000 miles, 2001 Audi TT that gets the mileage I needed, at the price I needed and is fun to drive.

You have to be willing to do what it takes, from menial, tedious steps, to having the patience for plans to come together. You also have to be willing to take big leaps when needed.

I will put up with the rain to get rainbows. How about you? Don't let discomfort stop you!

For all sad words of tongue and pen, the saddest are these, 'It might have been'. John Greenleaf Whittier

It's great to have dreams. But one needs to live their dreams . . . in spite of whatever problems, obstacles, or Negative Nellies that crop up.

When I do counseling, I ask the people to build a plan, not just to achieve their goals, but how they will handle the problems. I do this because with a plan on how you'll handle the problems, the naysayers, will almost always get you past the problem.

I mentioned how many people told me I was crazy to go to South America. I knew it would happen. I decided I would not let them intimidate me nor stop me. I decided I would go down there and make up my mind for myself. I'm glad I did.

Age is a matter of feeling...not of years. George William Curtis

I would be remiss if I didn't mention age. Age and aging is a reality. Like the bumper sticker says, 'Getting old ain't for sissies.'

But don't use it as an excuse and don't call it a reason for not going for your goals, your dreams.

I had a great aunt, who was in her eighties. She once lamented to me she didn't know why she was still alive when all of her family and most of her friends had passed away and her health was failing. I told her that as long as she was breathing, her reason for being on earth wasn't over. When we discussed that, we found the reason and it rejuvenated her and she lived a number of years more.

The only limits to the possibilities in your life tomorrow are the buts you use today. Les Brown

I love this guy. Talk about an overcomer, he overcame so many difficulties, over and over and over.

He did it by not limiting himself, and not sitting on his 'buts.'

If you do what you've always done, you'll get what you've always gotten. – Albert Einstein

I had always thought the strongest human drive was the sex drive. However, I read somewhere that wasn't true. The strongest drive was to remain in our comfort zones. When I read it, I thought it could very well be true. We don't like change. We like the status quo.

Yet, no progress has ever been made from the comfort zone. No progress has ever been made while sitting on the couch watching soaps, letting TV control our lives.

It's not enough to get out of your comfort zone. It requires different thinking, asking different questions, building a different attitude and very importantly, taking action.

What are you waiting for?

Man's mind, once stretched by a new idea, never regains its original dimensions. Oliver Wendell Holmes, Jr.

Folks, this is a big one. When you open your mind to different ideas, different ways of thinking, different cultures, you can't go back to where you were. Doesn't happen.

When I met my wife I knew she was a dog lover. However, I found out she had always wanted a show dog and to enter that world. I don't think she felt it would ever happen. I decided she should have a show dog for Christmas, but almost no one wanted to sell her a dog because she didn't have any credentials or experience. The few that would sell her one had such ludicrous demands that it didn't make sense to buy from them. Then she expanded her search and found a puppy in Sweden.

We talked, and when I said lets use a credit card and go for it. She said but what if I get there and the puppy isn't a show dog? I said then you'll know. If you don't go you will always wonder. The next problem was which of her two daughters to take to help her. I said you can't take just one, you need to take them both.

I tell this story because of the change it made in her and her two daughters. They didn't even have passports when we decided to go for it. The girls had never been on an airplane. None of them had ever been to another country.

A mind once opened never goes back to where it was. Especially neural pathways that find out doors can be opened and opportunities made!

I think everyone should have to visit another country and I don't mean going to an all inclusive resort. See the people, learn the culture and find that there are different ways of thinking. Open your mind!!!

It's the constant and determined effort that breaks down all resistance and sweeps away all obstacles. Claude M. Bristol

I once met an author, Og Mandino. At one time he was living the American dream with a good job, home in the burbs, a wife and 2 daughters. However, he became an alcoholic. He lost it all.

He ended up living in the back of an old car in middle America, in the winter. During a sleet storm he decided he had nothing to live for. He was living by panhandling and he went out and started begging. Not for money for food. Not for money for booze. He wanted enough money to buy a gun he saw in a pawnshop so he could end his life.

When he got up the next morning he had the money, but the store was closed. The only place open to get warm was the library. He went in. While there he saw a book, 'The Success System That Never Fails' by W. Clement Stone (remember that name?).

Og thought, "What bunk." He took the book down and started reading. It changed his outlook. He decided he wanted to work for Stone's company, to eventually work directly for Stone.

He went to the nearest office of Stone's company, which by the way sold insurance. He asked for a job. They kicked him out. They knew he was a bum. He went back again. They kicked him out again, and again, and again, and again, and again, six times. They finally decided to hire him, knowing that he wouldn't make it, 80% of the people hired in that industry don't make it.

He became a top earner. Went on to the company's bottom office and turned it around. He ended up being editor for the company's magazine, Success Magazine, which you might have seen on the shelf at bookstores.

Constant, determined effort! Doing what it takes to make your dreams happen. I've said it before: strong desire and taking action will get you going. However, don't look down on perseverance.

You get knocked down, get back up. Keep putting one foot in front of the other. Because a year from now you will either be where you are at today or you will be on the way to your dream OR possibly your dream will have come true. Don't stop!

The difference between a successful person and others is not a lack of strength, not a lack of knowledge, but rather in a lack of will. Vincent T. Lombardi

If you don't set goals, you'll be helping someone else achieve their goals. I don't know where I heard that, but I took it to heart.

As for strength, you can hire muscle. Knowledge? You can learn what you need to or hire someone who knows what you need to know.

You can buy, barter or get whatever you need except will. That has to come from within and it needs to be a burning desire.

There are two major ways to do this.

One, build a burning picture of what you want, so vivid that you can see it, taste it, touch it. A picture so strong that you can't live without it.

Two, you become disgusted with where you are at and **decide no more**. Build a picture of how bad this is and that you can't live this way anymore. Decide no more.

Then do whatever it takes to move away from this and move forward to a better life.

Where there is a will (think burning desire), there is a way.

The victory of success is half won when one gains the habit of setting goals and achieving them. Even the most tedious chore will become endurable as you parade through each day convinced that every task, no matter how menial or boring, brings you closer to fulfilling your dreams. Og Mandino

Set little goals, achieve them. Set bigger goals, achieve them. That's one way to build the success habit.

When I went to Colombia, I chose to make a big one and make it happen. I did it with a burning desire. Desire to travel. Desire to see more of the world. The desire to help make other's lives better.

Do whichever way works best for you. Do whichever way works best for you. Do whichever way works best for you. Make it come true my friend, make it come true.

When you have exhausted all possibilities, remember this - you haven't. Thomas Edison

Folks, as we get older, there are some things we just can't do anymore. However, not as many as you think.

There are a lot of seniors that learn new trades, new skills, get new jobs.

There are seniors who have worked out to have body builder bodies.

There are many who have moved to other countries so they can live better on the social security.

There are seniors who run marathons.

We may be senior citizens. We may be on medications. We may have aches and pains. But we must never be counted out. We still have dreams and we can live them if we so desire!

(And you young folk, this goes for you too. There are always options, there are always new doors, new windows, new fences you can go over, under, around, or through.)

Would you like me to give you a formula for...success? It's quite simple, really. Double your rate of failure... You're thinking of failure as the enemy of success. But it isn't at all... You can be discouraged by failure -- or you can learn from it. So go ahead and make mistakes. Make all you can. Because, remember that's where you'll find success. On the far side of failure. Thomas J. Watson

Did you know even most diehard baseball fans don't know the name of baseball player who held the record for the most strike outs. Do you? It was Babe Ruth! What? Yeah, but that isn't what he's remembered for, now is it?

Remember Colonel Sanders, 1,000 noes before he made a sale. How about Thomas Edison, 10,000 tries before he had a workable light bulb.

Made a mistake? Deal with it and move on.

Can you have a pity party? If you must, but make it short, make it a real party, then move onward and forward.

When defeat comes, accept it as a signal that your plans are not sound, rebuild those plans, and set sail once more toward your coveted goal. Napoleon Hill

I wanted to go to Mexico as a volunteer. I ended up in Colombia. Turned out to be the best thing that could have happened.

Be willing to change, especially as new information indicates it is the best choice. There is no progress in 'this is the way its always been done' or 'not invented here.'

By the way, 'not invented here' means not accepting ideas from others. Some of the best ideas I've seen came from little children because they haven't built boxes nor walls yet. Be open to new ideas, new ways of thinking and doing things. You'll be surprised.

Nothing is impossible; there are ways that lead to everything, and if we had sufficient will we should always have sufficient means. It is often merely for an excuse that we say things are impossible.
Francois De La Rochefoucauld

Take this part of the quote: If we had sufficient will we should always have sufficient means. I think this means burning desire. Now go back and reread the quote.

Think about this quote. I'm not saying this has to be one of your three quotes, but let it open doors to your mind, to the possibilities of your life.

'Plan your work, work your plan'

'Poor planning is planning for poor results'

'Planning without action is futile, action without planning is fatal'

'The method of the enterprising is to plan with audacity and execute with vigor'

'To be prepared is half the victory'

Folks, are there times to wing it? Maybe. But I can tell you that way too often I've shown up someplace without reservations and couldn't find a place to stay. Make plans.

Do plans sometimes go awry. Oh yeah. Still, it is easier to overcome problems when you had a plan that when you didn't. Just makes sense.

You cannot escape the results of your thoughts.... Whatever your present environment may be, you will fall, remain or rise with your thoughts, your vision, your ideal. You will become as small as your controlling desire, as great as your dominant aspiration. James Lane Allen

Choose wisely!

Before a painter puts a brush to his canvas he sees his picture mentally.... If you think of yourself in terms of a painting, what do you see? ... Is the picture one you think worth painting? ... You create yourself in the image you hold in your mind. Thomas Dreier

Makeovers aren't just for the young. Makeovers aren't just for women. Makeovers aren't just a new hairdo.

You can get a new wardrobe. Get a new hairdo. Get a new job or even move to a new city. But that isn't a makeover, those things are just lifestyle changes.

To really have a makeover, you need to change the way you think. When you have a positive attitude, an overcomer belief and can-do reframing mindset, then you've taken the first and most important step towards a makeover.

To help me to do that, I bought my Audi TT. I use it as a mnemonic, to remind me of my new goals and what I want to accomplish as I finish this year and move towards next year with a can-do attitude. Plus it's fun to drive.

Can you use clothes to do the same thing? Yes, as long as you see that as a tool to help you with your new mindset. The same for a new hairdo, a new job, or a new move. Make it work for you, remembering that when you paint the picture of who you want to be, an attitude adjustment is the first step.

Sit down, plan who you want to be, where you want to go, then plan on what you must do to paint that picture, to be who you want to be. Go forth and paint your life with beautiful vibrant colors!!!

End Game

I will leave you with this. William James, a pioneering American psychologist and philosopher trained as a medical doctor, said, ***"Human beings can alter their lives by altering their attitudes of mind."***

Excerpt from the book, 'The Melee Method Way to Weigh Less':

'If someone you trust were to come to you with cupped hands and say, "I have within my hands the key that will open the door to your success. What will you give me for it?"

What would such a key be worth to you? What if you didn't have enough money in the bank? Would you be willing to sell something you own to obtain this key? Would you be willing to go into debt to obtain this key? Think about it, THE KEY THAT OPENS THE DOOR TO SUCCESS! What would such a key be worth? What is the potential value you could get with such a key?

Ahhh, but you have already made the investment. By owning this book you will now receive the key, as part of our agreement to take you on a journey towards achieving your dream. Note though, before you receive this key: it opens the door to your success, but it does not guarantee your success, that dear friend is another key. What? You will have to wait a bit for that key, but this key, THE KEY THAT OPENS THE DOOR TO SUCCESS, is a key called ATTITUDE!'

As Zig Ziglar says, **"Your attitude controls your altitude."**

I once purchased seven polo shirts of different colors. I then took them to a local business that does embroidery and had them write '**ATTITUDE is everything**' on the left sleeves. I still have most of them. That became my focus, my mantra, and as a reminder, helped me move to higher levels in my life.

As you can see, can feel, quotes have power. Quotes can have a number of levels of meaning if you look hard enough. However, most of all, I am hoping you have found that quotes have power, the power for you to make a difference in your life.

I have quotes, with pictures, hanging on the wall of my home office, lots of quotes. I use them as motivators. I use them as reminders. I use them to overcome negatives when I'm feeling down. The main idea here is that I USE them.

Please pick your quotes wisely. It doesn't take three. One good one will work. A number of them, from different genres, can open your mind up to new thinking.

No matter the number, the key is to USE them to make the difference you want to in YOUR life!

I wish you the best!!!

PS: One of my favorite quotes I have framed on my wall, that has impacted me immensely. is this one by Ferdinand Magellan, **"The sea is dangerous and its storms terrible, but these obstacles have never been sufficient reason to remain ashore...unlike the mediocre, intrepid spirits seek victory over those things that seem impossible...it is with an iron will that they embark on the most daring of all endeavors...to meet the shadowy future without fear and conquer the unknown."**

3 Quotes CAN Make a Difference . . .

Index

www.ingramcontent.com/pod-product-compliance
Lightning Source LLC
Chambersburg PA
CBHW070813050426
42452CB00011B/2021